THE METROPOLITAN LINE

Reprinted April 1973

I.S.B.N. 0 85329 033 4

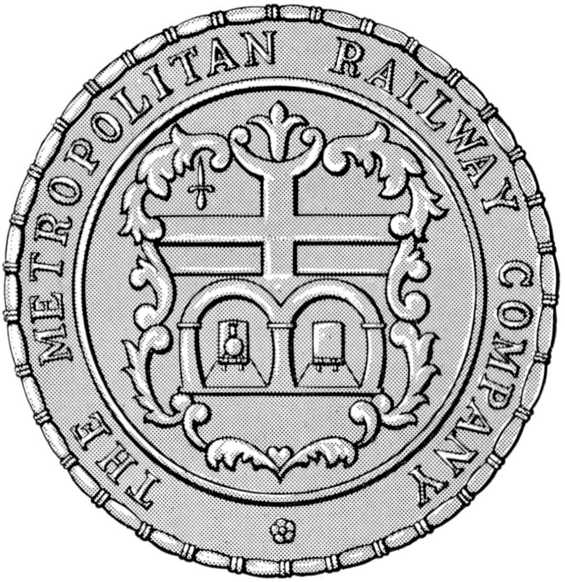

1 Seal of the Metropolitan Railway Company including the arms of the City of London (St. George's Cross with the Sword of St. Paul). The seal showed the trains in reverse positions, in accordance with heraldic convention

2 Device used by the Metropolitan Railway in the twentieth century. To the Arms of the City of London have been added those of Middlesex, Buckinghamshire, and Hertfordshire

The Metropolitan Line

by

Charles E. Lee, F.C.I.T.

LONDON TRANSPORT
55 Broadway, Westminster, S.W.1.

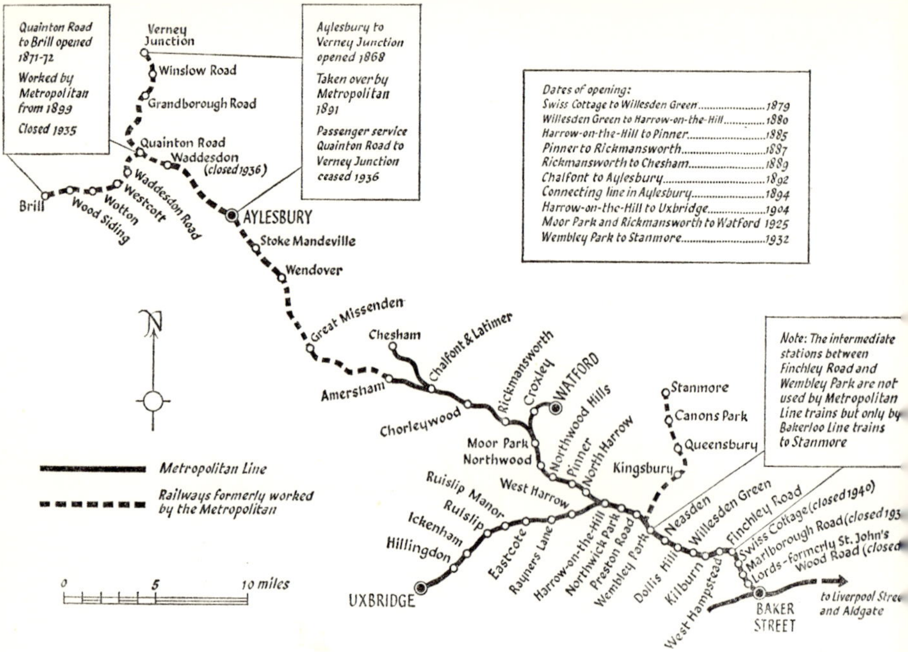

The Metropolitan 'Extension Line'

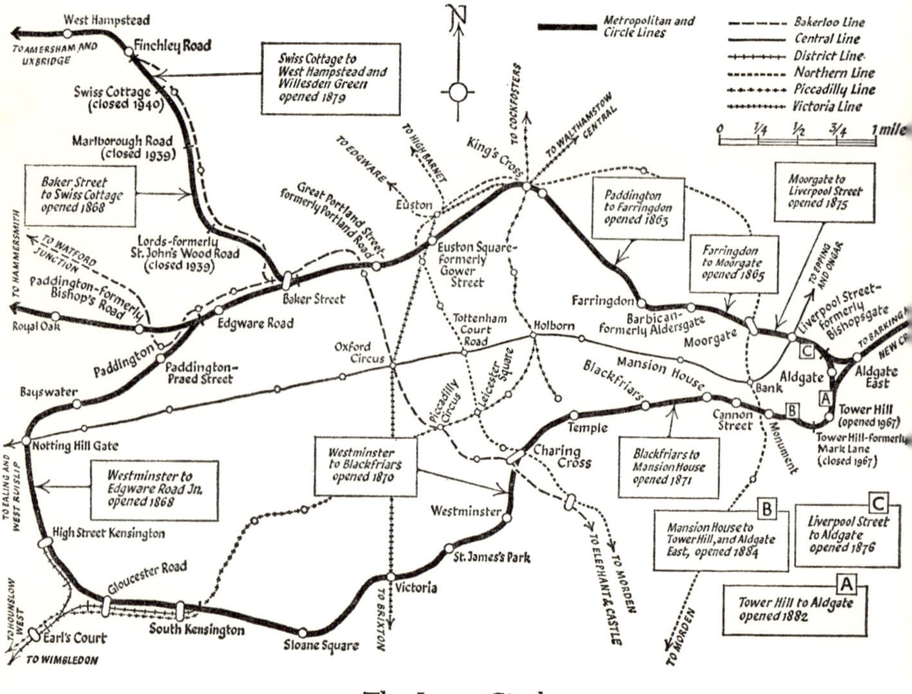

The Inner Circle

Illustrations

Frontispiece: *1. Seal of the Metropolitan Railway Company*
2. Device used by the Metropolitan Railway

1. *Machine for hoisting excavated earth, 1861*
2. *Excavating in Praed Street in 1866*
3. *Trial trip on 24 May 1862 in broad-gauge trucks*
4. *Another trial trip, on 30 August 1862 – passing Portland Road Station*
5. *The first public train at Bishop's Road, Metropolitan Railway*
6. *The* ILLUSTRATED LONDON NEWS *of 27 December 1862; completed stations*
7. *Farringdon Street Station in March 1866*
8. *Entrance to Clerkenwell Tunnel in 1868*
9. *The original King's Cross Station under construction in 1862*
10. *Interior of King's Cross Station in 1862*
11. *King's Cross – Gray's Inn Road frontage in 1910*
12. *Broad-gauge train at Praed Street Junction*
13. *Scene outside Aldgate Station about 1902*
14. *Bayswater Station on its completion*
15. *Notting Hill Gate Station in 1868*
16. *One of the original entrances to Baker Street Station*
17. *Baker Street Station in 1933*

between pages 12 and 13

18. *Harrow Station, opened on 2 August 1880*
19. *Harrow-on-the-Hill in September 1960*
20. *Rayners Lane Station in February 1933*
21. *The rebuilt Rayners Lane Station at the time of its opening on 8 August 1938*
22. *The original terminus of the Uxbridge branch opened on 4 July 1904*
23. *Inaugural train of the Uxbridge branch at Ruislip*

Illustrations *continued*

24. Uxbridge Station opened on 4 December 1938

25. A surburban Metropolitan Railway train near Willesden Green

26. Six-coach headed by 'E' class steam locomotive at Neasden in 1905

27. 'K' class locomotive on 'main-line' train, including a Pullman coach

28. One of the first (1864) batch of 'A' class 4-4-0 tank locomotives

29. 'G' class 0-6-4 tank locomotive built in 1916 for express passenger work

30. Camel-back electric locomotive No. 1

31. Electric Metropolitan Railway locomotives

32. Rear view of later Metropolitan Railway multiple-unit electric stock

33. Five-coach Circle at South Kensington in October 1950

34. A train of new 'A 60' stock

35. 'C 69' stock designed for Circle Line and Hammersmith & City workings

36 and 37. Compartment stock for 'main-line' service; first-class and third-class accommodation

38. Interior of 'C 69' in 1970

between pages 20 and 21

The Metropolitan Line

When the Metropolitan Railway opened to public traffic on Saturday, 10 January 1863, its 3¾-mile line from Paddington (Bishop's Road) to Farringdon Street, London was given the first urban underground railway in the world, and some 40,000 persons were carried on the opening day.

The idea of such a line was one of gradual evolution. As early as 1845 a project was formed for uniting the Great Western Railway at Paddington with the Eastern Counties Railway at Shoreditch by means of a tunnel under the New Road. Despite the fact that Robert Stephenson was the engineer, nothing came of this scheme, but from that period the advocacy of a railway tunnel under this great east-west thoroughfare continued. The New Road, which made such a project practicable without vast demolition of houses, was evolved in 1755 by 'some gentlemen of the greatest eminence and property in the County of Middlesex' to provide the first by-pass road in London, partly to avoid driving cattle along Oxford Street and Holborn to Smithfield Market. It was to extend from Paddington to Islington, and thus afford a route which 'in times of threatened invasion would form a complete line of circumvallation, and His Majesty's forces could then easily and expeditiously march that way into Essex to defend our coasts, without passing through the cities of London and Westminster.' Despite some opposition, it was sanctioned by Parliament on 27 May 1756; built with commendable promptitude; and opened in September of the same year. A series of Orders dated 20 February 1857 abolished the century-old name New Road, and legally established Marylebone Road, Euston Road, and Pentonville Road.

A separate approach to the problem of improving railway access to the City of London arose from the desire to clear the squalid and insanitary area in the valley of the River Fleet. The first part of Farringdon Street, from Ludgate Circus to Holborn Hill, had been opened in August 1830, and in 1838 the City Corporation was empowered to extend this road northward to Clerkenwell Green. The Clerkenwell Improvement Commission, with wider objects, was formed in 1840, but progress was slow, by reason of financial stringency. During the Railway Mania period of the 1840s, proposals were made for a railway in a covered way along the Fleet valley, which would function as a Grand Central Terminus for railways from the north, bringing them to the City of London itself. This idea was warmly welcomed, if indeed not originated, by Charles Pearson (1793-1862), who had become Solicitor to the Corporation of the City of London in 1839, and it was his enthusiasm and unflagging advocacy which refused to let the scheme die and was largely responsible for ultimate achievement. None of the early proposals survived, but the improved outlook of the Great Exhibition year of 1851 enabled Pearson to advocate a revised Fleet Valley scheme in November 1851, which became the City Terminus Company. His inclusion in the plans of broad-gauge tracks showed that he envisaged an ultimate link with the Great Western Railway at Paddington. Isambard Kingdom Brunel, the famous engineer who built the present Paddington main-line station in 1851-54, is stated to have adopted the level at which it stands partly because he 'felt convinced that one day there would be an underground railway running round London at about that level.'

The successful scheme which became the nucleus of the Metropolitan Railway was formed under the name of the Bayswater, Paddington & Holborn Bridge Railway, the directors of which held their first meeting on 10 January 1853, exactly ten years before the railway was opened to the public, and appointed John Fowler as their engineer. By the time that the company's scheme had secured Parliamentary approval, the title had been changed to the North Metropolitan Railway, and this was used in the Act of incorporation which received the Royal Assent on 15 August 1853. This authorized a line between Paddington and King's Cross only, but the promoters joined forces with the City Terminus Company which intended initially to link King's Cross with Holborn Bridge (Farringdon Street), and the whole project was reincorporated as the Metropolitan Railway on 7 August 1854. The enlarged plan received the financial support of the Great Western Railway, which desired access to the City. For some years the building of the line remained in abeyance, as it proved impossible to raise enough capital. Apart from the Crimean War and general depression, the general public did not take kindly to the idea of travelling underground and would not subscribe money for such an enterprise. A prospectus issued in July 1856 failed to attract sufficient support, but Charles Pearson did not relax his efforts. At a public meeting held on 1 December 1858 he advocated 'the provision of cheap railway accommodation to enable the working classes to reside in their adjacent country districts,' and in April 1859 persuaded the City Corporation to take an interest in the undertaking to the extent of a £200,000 subscription, or one fifth of the intended capital of one million pounds. The Great Western Railway subscribed £175,000 and by the end of 1859 the whole capital had been obtained.

In December 1859 construction contracts were awarded to Smith & Knight for the portion from Euston Square to Paddington, and to John Jay for the section from Euston Square to 'Victoria Street'. The last-named was that portion of Farringdon Street outside the City boundary; it was re-named Farringdon Road on 22 May 1863. At the beginning of February 1860 it was announced that shafts were being sunk at several places along the line. One had been opened on an unoccupied piece of land at King's Cross, and another near Euston Square. The form of construction, although often loosely called tunnelling, was mainly cut-and-cover. This consisted of digging a trench, supporting the soil with side walls, roofing over the railway track, and restoring the road surface. As the railway was designed to accommodate double tracks of mixed gauge (the standard 4 ft. $8\frac{1}{2}$ in. as used on most railways, and the 7 ft. $0\frac{1}{4}$ in. broad gauge of the G.W.R.), much of the covered way comprised a six-ring elliptical brick arch of 28 ft. 6 in. span, above vertical side walls three bricks thick with a rise of 11 ft. From rail level to the springing of the arch was 5 ft. 6 in. No invert was built and no concrete was placed under the 4-ft. wide footings. Ordinary stock bricks and blue lias or greystone lime were used throughout. Where the depth was not sufficient for a brick-arched way, brick and concrete side walls in 8-ft. bays of piers and recesses were built. The roof was then provided by cast-iron girders from 1 ft. 6 in. to 2 ft. 6 in. deep, spaced 6 ft. to 8 ft. apart. Between King's Cross and Farringdon Street much of the work was left in open cutting, but this section also included the Clerkenwell tunnel, the only true tunnel on the original line. It was 728 yd. long, was begun in November 1860, and finished in May 1862. In addition to the main line, tunnel links with the Great Northern Railway were made at King's Cross.

John (afterwards Sir John) Fowler (1817-1898) was the Engineer-in-Chief and Thomas Marr Johnson (1826-1876) the Resident Engineer. Fowler was a man of intense self-reliance, as well as the possessor of considerable technical skill, and both were taxed in the execution of this pioneer engineering achievement. The original contracts required the railway to be completed in 21 months, and work was pursued energetically throughout 1860, aided by an elaborate 'machine for hoisting up the earth from below'. At times it involved closing a section of the public road and diverting the traffic. A portion of the unfinished cutting, 'near Tunbridge Place, New Road,' fell in on Friday, 24 May 1861, carrying away the pavement, gardens, telegraph wires, gas mains, and New River water mains. The damage was mainly repaired within a week. A report on progress in September 1861 said that 'between Portland Road and Euston Square navvies swarm like bees in a hive'.

Trial trips were made over finished parts of the line on 28 November 1861 and 'no doubt whatever was entertained that the line would be opened for traffic in April or May next'. It was hoped to benefit from the expected heavy traffic in connection with the Great Exhibition of 1862, but this proved to be far too optimistic. The first trial trip over the whole line was made on 24 May 1862 in trucks provided by Smith & Knight, and the distinguished party included the Rt. Hon. William Ewart Gladstone, at that time Chancellor of the Exchequer. A July opening was then mentioned, but, on Wednesday 18 June the Fleet Ditch Sewer burst into the works in Farringdon Street and filled them to a depth of 10 ft. as far as King's Cross. By 6 August nearly all the damage had been repaired, and an opening on 1 October was expected. Another trial train was run on 30 August with shareholders, after an inspection by the Government Inspector of Railways earlier in the day.

On Monday 22 December, Colonel Yolland made his formal inspection on behalf of the Board of Trade, which until 1919 was the Department responsible for the supervision of public railways. He then required signalling alterations, and again inspected on 30 December, when he gave his general approval. The final Board of Trade inspection was conducted by Colonel Yolland on 3 January 1863, and thence until the 8th a 'ghost' service of empty trains was run so as to test the signalling and accustom the members of the staff to their work.

In November 1861 the Great Western Railway had agreed to work the line, supplying locomotive power and rolling stock, and initially it was therefore broad-gauge stock specially provided for the underground service which was employed. On Friday 9 January 1863 the directors and a party of some 600 travelled from Bishop's Road to Farringdon Street in two trains, leaving soon after 1 p.m. and taking 2 h. 10 min., as lengthy stops were made to view the stations at Edgware Road, Baker Street, Portland Road, and the 'beautiful and spacious station at King's Cross'. It is believed that the guests numbered about 350, and that the remainder were shareholders and others associated with the company. At Farringdon Street, in a specially-built temporary hall 250 ft. long and 50 ft. wide, a banquet was served and many speeches were delivered.

With the inauguration of public traffic the next day, extraordinary scenes were witnessed at the stations in consequence of the keen desire of the public to experience the new means of transit. The original timetable provided for 67 trains each way on weekdays, and 48 on Sundays, stopping at all stations, and taking 18 min. for the journey of $3\frac{3}{4}$ miles. The service interval was every 15 min. from 8 a.m. to 8 p.m. with additional trains on weekdays at 20 min. headway from 6 to 8 a.m.

and 8 to 12 p.m. and 8 to 10.40 p.m. on Sundays. On Sunday morning there was the customary suspension of service during church hours, a practice which survived on the Metropolitan until 3 October 1909. All trains accommodated first, second, and third class passengers, and the three classes survived on the Metropolitan until 17 December 1906. The five intermediate stations were Edgware Road (a spelling which was alternated with Edgeware Road in the original timetable); Baker Street; Portland Road (this station became Great Portland Street only on 1 March 1917, but the thoroughfare had made the change on 13 November 1863); Gower Street (renamed Euston Square on 1 November 1909); and King's Cross.

Charles Pearson had the satisfaction of seeing the railway built, but he died on 14 September 1862, in his 69th year, before public traffic was begun. At the time of his death, the directors of the railway had recorded their appreciation of 'the very valuable services so long and cheerfully rendered by him to this company without fee or reward' and, shortly after the opening, as soon as revenue was being received, they granted an annuity of £250 to his widow.

For working the Metropolitan Railway, Daniel Gooch of the G.W.R. designed some outside-cylinder 2–4–0 broad-gauge tank engines, with condensing apparatus, of which 22 were built. The coupled wheels were 6 ft. in dia. and the leading wheels 3 ft. 6 in. The cylinders were 16 in. by 24 ins There was no protection of any kind for the engine crew, as it was feared that condensation on glass would obscure the view. The rolling stock supplied by the G.W.R. comprised 45 eight-wheel compartment carriages of a uniform length of 42 ft. over buffers. The four axles were grouped in pairs at each end, but they were not bogies. Six were old stock, but the remainder (6 first, 9 composite first and second, 10 second, and 14 third class) were new vehicles 10 ft. 6 in. wide, with teak bodies, built by Brown & Marshalls of Birmingham. These carriages were coal gas lighted, and (excepting for experimental vehicles) were the first to be so equipped. The gas was not compressed, but was contained in collapsible bags or bellows on the roof of the carriage.

Signalling was of the mechanical type common at the period,

1 Machine for hoisting excavated earth from the Metropolitan Railway cutting in the Euston Road (From the *Illustrated Times* 19 October 1861)

2 Excavating in Praed Street near Paddington Station in 1866. The Metropolitan station was opened as Paddington (Praed Street) on 1 October 1868; it was renamed Paddington on 11 July 1948 *Charles E. Lee*

3 Trial trip on 24 May 1862 in broad-gauge trucks of Smith & Knight, contractors. The distinguished party included W. E. Gladstone

4 Another trial trip, on 30 August 1862. The train is seen passing Portland Road Station, which was renamed Great Portland Street on 1 March 1917

5 The first public train at Bishop's Road, Metropolitan Railway, on 10 January 1863, as depicted in the *Illustrated Times*

6 Stations of the completed railway as shown in the *Illustrated London News* of 27 December 1862

7 Farringdon Street Station in March 1866 with part of the 'Widened Lines' in use

8 Entrance to Clerkenwell Tunnel in 1868, showing the 'Widened Lines' passing under the original tracks

9 The original King's Cross Station, Metropolitan Railway, under construction in 1862

10 Interior of King's Cross Station in 1862

11 The station was extensively reconstructed in 1910-11 in connection with the building of a new street called King's Cross Bridge (opened 29 June 1912), and the high-arch all-over roof was demolished. This view shows the Gray's Inn Road frontage in 1910, the year of the Japan-British Exhibition at White City, shortly before the demolition. For Circle Line trains it was replaced by a new station further west on 14 March 1941

12 Broad-gauge train at Praed Street junction as shown on a contemporary lithograph

13 Scene outside Aldgate Station about 1902

14 Bayswater Station on its completion. It was opened on 1 October 1868. This exterior is representative of the style of architecture adopted by the Metropolitan Railway at this period *Charles E. Lee*

15 Notting Hill Gate Station looking towards Bayswater in 1868. The station was rebuilt in 1956-60 as a joint station serving the Circle and Central Lines *Charles E. Lee*

16 One of the original entrances to Baker Street Station in the early years of the century. The horse bus was owned by the London Road-Car Co. Ltd. which flew the Union Jack as a distinctive symbol

17 Baker Street Station in 1933 when the Metropolitan became part of London Transport. A long overdue rebuilding had been undertaken in 1911 and the 'centre stone' (on the plinth in the foreground) was laid on 24 July 1912. Chiltern Court flats, over the station, and intended originally as an hotel, were built in 1929-30

but the Metropolitan was the first railway to be worked throughout on the absolute block system. All points and signals were interlocked. The installation was the first occasion on which the block telegraph instruments introduced by C. E. Spagnoletti, the Telegraph Superintendent of the G.W.R., were used; they later became standard on the Great Western. It is of interest to note that, at the time of the appointment in 1874 of the Royal Commission to inquire into the safety of railway working, the Metropolitan and the District were the only railways in the United Kingdom to have both interlocking and block working throughout.

Friction soon arose between the Metropolitan and the G.W.R. on both financial and operating matters. The one of greatest interest to the travelling public was that the Metropolitan desired more frequent trains than the four an hour, but the Great Western officers feared loss of money by more intensive working. The Great Western gave notice on 18 July 1863 that it would cease to work the railway at the end of September, and the Metropolitan replied that it would take it over on 1 October. In retaliation, the Great Western said that its rolling stock would be withdrawn on 10 August. Myles (afterwards Sir Myles) Fenton, the General Manager of the Metropolitan (which he had joined as operating superintendent in May 1862) found himself in the position of having to find within about ten days sufficient locomotives and carriages to work the line. In this emergency he threw himself upon the generosity of the Great Northern and the London & North Western, and from both these companies obtained the loan of carriages.

Suitable locomotives were not so easy to find, as the Metropolitan was precluded from using those emitting steam and smoke. Archibald Sturrock, the Locomotive Superintendent of the G.N.R. (and a former Manager of Swindon Works), had already prepared at Doncaster a few smoke-condensing locomotives for the suburban service which the G.N.R. had intended to extend over the Metropolitan from King's Cross to Farringdon Street on 1 September. Some other engines he now adapted within the time available by fitting them with a pipe and flexible tube leading from the exhaust pipe of the engine to the tender, and about a dozen in all were provided.

When the rolling stock was thus obtained, however, a new difficulty presented itself. The mixed-gauge tracks (standard and 7 ft.) had been provided by three rails. The one nearest to the platform was common to both, so that trains came alongside the platform face. An outer rail was 7 ft. away, for broad-gauge trains, and an intermediate rail would accommodate standard-gauge trains. This 'middle rail' (which had never been used) was found to be defective. Consequently, the first few days of the new arrangements were a time of great anxiety to all concerned. The G.W.R. broad-gauge trains maintained the service on Monday, 10 August, and the temporary standard-gauge trains began working on Tuesday, 11 August. After the initial teething troubles, all difficulties were surmounted successfully.

On 1 October (a month later than intended) the Great Northern 'suburban and City' service was begun. The passengers by the first through train to Farringdon Street are said to have expressed their delight by swooping down in force upon the refreshment buffet, newly-opened, and consuming all it contained. Henceforth the Metropolitan worked its own traffic with standard-gauge stock, but, as soon as the differences between the companies had been composed, in the autumn, the Great Western began to run through some broad-gauge trains between Windsor and Farringdon Street, and later worked a broad-gauge service on the Hammersmith line for a short time, and then between Addison Road and the City, so that the large carriages, for which their great carrying capacity was so eminently suited, were not yet entirely banished from the line. Broad-gauge trains were finally withdrawn on 15 March 1869.

Immediate steps were taken by the Metropolitan to secure its own locomotives and rolling stock. An initial order was placed with Beyer, Peacock & Co. in October 1863 for 18 steam-condensing locomotives of the 4–4–0 side-tank variety, and this was the basic design for practically all engines used until electrification. The original livery was dark green, but this was changed to chocolate brown about 1885. Much of the detail work in design was carried out by Robert Harvey Burnett, at that time a Beyer, Peacock pupil, and it was on the strength of this that he was appointed the first Locomotive

Superintendent of the Metropolitan, a position which he held until 1872. The first of the new engines was delivered on 20 June 1864 and the last on 27 August. As only 12 were necessary for working the timetable, the Metropolitan was able to dispense with its borrowed locomotives by the end of July.

Passenger carriages of the compartment type were ordered, and sufficient had been delivered by June 1864 to enable borrowed vehicles to be returned. The new stock was similar in design to that which had been used by the Great Western Railway, but was narrower as it was for the standard gauge. The detailed development of the rolling stock is not dealt with in the present booklet, as it is well covered in the publication 'Steam to Silver', an illustrated history of London Transport surface railway rolling stock by J. Graeme Bruce.

Meanwhile, extensions of the original line at both ends had been authorized. The Metropolitan itself secured its Finsbury Circus Extension Act on 6 August 1861, but this projection of the system eastwards to Moorgate Street was not opened until 23 December 1865. Westward, a line to Hammersmith (using the G.W.R. between Bishop's Road and Westbourne Park) was promoted by a separate company. This was the Hammersmith & City Railway, incorporated on 22 July 1861, to build a mixed-gauge line from Green Lane Junction (Westbourne Park) to Hammersmith, with a branch from Latimer Road to Uxbridge Road on the West London Railway. The line to Hammersmith was opened on 13 June 1864, and passenger traffic consisted of an extension at half-hourly intervals of the Farringdon Street to Bishop's Road service. It was worked entirely by the G.W.R. with broad-gauge locomotives and carriages until 1 April 1865, when the Metropolitan took over the service with standard-gauge stock. The Hammersmith & City undertaking was vested in the G.W.R. and Metropolitan jointly by Act of 15 July 1867. The broad-gauge rail was removed between Hammersmith and Latimer Road in August 1868, and between Uxbridge Road and Westbourne Park on 15 March 1869.

The successful opening of the Metropolitan Railway coincided with revived activity in the promotion of railway schemes for the Metropolis, and in 1864 there were no fewer than 259 different projects for making about 300 miles of railway in and about London. Early in the session of 1864 the schemes were referred to a joint committee of both Houses of Parliament, which advised that many should not be entertained. Four additional lines affecting the Metropolitan Railway were sanctioned, and all received their Acts on the same date. Three concerned the completion of an Inner Circle, and the fourth was the nucleus of what became the well-known 'Extension line' that ultimately reached Verney Junction and profoundly affected the history and objectives of the Metropolitan for much of its independent career.

Under the title of 'Metropolitan District Railways', a fully-developed scheme had been put forward in November 1863 by John Fowler for completing an Inner Circle, north of the Thames, and making an Outer Circle by means of a series of connecting lines of existing railways. The joint committee approved of the completion of the Inner Circle, and this portion of Fowler's scheme (consolidated with a rival scheme covering similar ground, called the Metropolitan Grand Union Railway) emerged successfully. The Metropolitan Railway (Notting Hill and Brompton Extension) Act of 29 July 1864 authorized the original Metropolitan company to extend its line from Paddington to South Kensington; and the Metropolitan Railway (Tower Hill Extension) Act of the same date sanctioned the line from Moorgate to the Minories, Tower Hill. The remainder of the Inner Circle, namely, South Kensington to Tower Hill, was granted to another company—the Metropolitan District Railway, invariably called the 'District'—together with spurs from South Kensington (duplicating the authorized Metropolitan line as far as Gloucester Road) to a junction with the West London Extension Railway at West Brompton; and from Kensington High Street to the West London Railway near Addison Road.

The western extension was opened on 1 October 1868 from Edgware Road to Gloucester Road (including the Campden Hill tunnel, 421 yd. long) and thence to South Kensington on 24 December 1868. On the latter date the District Railway (worked by the Metropolitan to 2 July 1871) was opened from South Kensington to Westminster Bridge; it was extended to Blackfriars on 30 May 1870, and to Mansion House on

3 July 1871. On the eastern extension (after considerable delays), the section was opened on 1 February 1875 from Moorgate to Liverpool Street (Great Eastern Railway),* and on 12 July of the same year from Liverpool Street Junction to Bishopsgate Metropolitan Station (renamed Liverpool Street on 1 November 1909). The spur to the Great Eastern Railway appears to have been used for the last time in 1904; it was disconnected in 1907 and removed in 1916. The Bishopsgate to Aldgate section was brought into use on 18 November 1876, and construction work was then suspended, leaving a gap in the Inner Circle between Aldgate and Mansion House.

The Metropolitan & St. John's Wood Railway, also incorporated on 29 July 1864, was a semi-independent company in which the Metropolitan had a considerable shareholding. The first section was opened as a single line on 13 April 1868 with stations at Baker Street Junction, St. John's Wood Road, Marlborough Road, and Swiss Cottage. The excavated soil was used to reduce the depth of the lake in Regent's Park, where some 40 persons had died in January 1867 when the ice gave way. A through railway service was maintained between Swiss Cottage and Moorgate from the opening until 7 March 1869, but thereafter the junction at Baker Street was not again used for passenger service until 28 January 1907, all 'Extension line' trains terminating at Baker Street. From Swiss Cottage to West Hampstead was opened on 30 June 1879, and thence to Willesden Green on 24 November 1879. The further extension to Harrow was brought into use on 2 August 1880, and a junction with the Midland Railway at Finchley Road, for goods traffic only, on 1 October 1880, but the original section between Baker Street and Swiss Cottage was not double tracked until 10 July 1882. The St. John's Wood company was vested in the Metropolitan as from 1 January 1883 by an Act of 3 July 1882.

In many respects, the Metropolitan was a pioneer, and one sphere in which it took the lead would have proved pleasing to Charles Pearson. This was in being the first London line

*The Great Eastern itself had been extended from its original terminus at Shoreditch to Liverpool Street only a short time before. Liverpool Street (G.E.R.) was opened to local traffic on 2 February 1874, and for all traffic on 1 November 1875.

to introduce workmen's fares, a step which it took in May 1864, well in advance of any Statutory obligation. At first the trains carried about 2,000 weekly in each direction, and the number gradually increased to 4,000. There were two trains each way, starting at 5.30 and 5.40 a.m. and the workmen were permitted to return by any train in the day for the return fare of 3d. The company was not compelled to provide any workmen's trains until the line was open to Moorgate, when it was required to run one train each way daily at a single fare of 1d.

The idea of Charles Pearson and his associates that the Metropolitan should provide a central terminal for main-line trains was never pursued, partly because a Parliamentary Select Committee in 1863 had reported 'that it would be objectionable to allow the construction of a great central station in the Metropolis', but suburban trains of numerous railways did use some portion of the Metropolitan to reach a city terminus. This had been foreseen from the outset, in view of the links with the G.W.R. at Paddington and the G.N.R. at King's Cross, and plans had been made for providing more tracks at the City end. The London, Chatham & Dover Railway had bridged the River Thames at Blackfriars in 1864 and reached Ludgate Hill. On 1 January 1866 it was extended to a junction with the Metropolitan at Farringdon Street, and established the first (and only) main-line railway link through the heart of London. It was used from the outset by G.N.R. and L.C.D.R. trains; by Midland trains from 1 June 1869; and by South Eastern trains from 1 August 1880. In the changed circumstances of new urban electric railways, and the coming of the motorbus, all such once-numerous through passenger services (which often took circuitous routes) were withdrawn in 1907 and 1908. The line remained in use for goods traffic for a further 60 years.

At this period the Midland Railway was building its London extension line to a terminus at St. Pancras, and the scheme also included an underground link with the Metropolitan at King's Cross. To meet the needs of these 'foreign' railways, the Metropolitan therefore embarked on what are called the 'Widened Lines', extending from King's Cross to terminal platforms at Moorgate Street. These separate tracks were brought into use between Farringdon Street and Aldersgate Street on 1 March 1866 and between Aldersgate Street and Moorgate Street on 1 July 1866. The remaining section, between King's Cross and Farringdon Street, involved heavier work, including a 'Widening' tunnel parallel with the Clerkenwell tunnel. This was begun in November 1865 and completed in May 1867. It was 733 yd. long, but deeper at the east end than the earlier one, as here the rails passed under the original line. The King's Cross link with the Great Northern was diverted to the 'Widened Lines' and a new link established with the low-level section of the Midland Railway. The new Metropolitan tracks between King's Cross and Farringdon Street were brought into use for goods traffic on 27 January 1868 and for passengers on 17 February. By this means, also, the Midland Railway was enabled to establish a local passenger service between Bedford and Moorgate Street on 13 July 1868. From the Midland Railway curve, a double-line tunnel was built for about 770 ft. westward with the intention of making a physical connection with the London & North Western Railway near Euston, but this was never done, and the works lay derelict for 58 years.

From the outset, the Metropolitan barred smoking in its carriages, to avoid adding to the difficulties of steam operation in tunnel. Not until 1868 was the general provision of smoking carriages on trains made compulsory. In July of that year, H. B. Sheridan, the Member for Dudley, moved an amendment to the Railway Regulation Bill requiring all railways, unless specially excused by the Board of Trade, to attach a smoking carriage to every train consisting of more than one carriage of each class. The amendment was warmly supported by John Stuart Mill in the last speech he delivered in the House of Commons, and it was largely the result of his advocacy that the clause was passed by a majority of 22. The Metropolitan Railway was specially excluded from the requirement and continued to endeavour to prevent smoking, but it was faced with the anomalous situation that trains of other companies on its lines were required to provide for smokers. Eventually it bowed to public demand and smoking carriages were first provided by the Metropolitan on 1 September 1874, although, as early as 6 September 1867, the journal *Engineering* had recorded that 'smoking is openly or tacitly allowed everywhere'.

In its early days the District Railway, which had built the southern part of the Inner Circle, was generally regarded as virtually part of the Metropolitan, which worked the line from the outset, as we have seen. It had, however, independent directors who became dissatisfied with the working, and they gave formal notice on 3 January 1870 of the intention to terminate the working agreement, to become effective on 3 July 1871. The Metropolitan directors on the District Board resigned and the District appointed its own Managing Director in the person of James Staats Forbes (1823-1904) who had been General Manager of the London, Chatham & Dover Railway since 1862, and continued in that office. Forbes became a director of the Chatham Company in 1871, and also Chairman of the District in 1872. It was a step that was to lead to the development of the District Railway, not only as an independent enterprise but also as the active (and at times bitter) competitor of its erstwhile parent.

At this time the financial position of the Metropolitan was deplorable and some of the proceedings of its Board had been characterised by the Court as "false, fictitious, and fraudulent." Eventually on 7 August 1872 Sir Edward William Watkin (1819-1901) was elected Chairman of the Metropolitan. Watkin had been Chairman of the South Eastern Railway since 1866 and already was known as a keen opponent of Forbes. Both men were extremely autocratic, and any reasonable co-operation between Metropolitan and District, or between S.E.R. and L.C.D.R., was outside the range of practical politics while both remained in their respective saddles. It is a subject of amazement to later generations that the personal magnetism and powers of leadership of the two men enabled them to carry with them their respective bodies of shareholders, while they expended their great powers in the interests of their own ambitions and careers and in personal rivalry.

Although the two companies had been empowered by Parliament to complete an Inner Circle, the idea very soon appeared unattractive to them, and particularly to the Metropolitan. Personal enmity between Watkin and Forbes was an important factor in delaying the completion of the

18 Harrow Station was opened on 2 August 1880, and renamed Harrow-on-the-Hill on 1 June 1894. It was enlarged to four platforms on 21 June 1908, and was the principal locomotive change point from 19 July 1908 until 1925

19 Harrow-on-the-Hill in September 1960. The station was rebuilt in 1938-39 as part of the extensive 1935/1940 New Works Programme, but had not been finished on the outbreak of war. It was finished in January 1943

20 Rayners Lane Station was opened as a halt on 26 May 1906. The word halt was later dropped. This view was taken in February 1933

21 The rebuilt Rayners Lane Station at the time of its opening on 8 August 1938. Until a few years earlier, the surrounding country had been pasture land. Even in 1930 only some 22,000 passengers a year used Rayners Lane; in 1937 it was 4,000,000

22 The original terminus of the Uxbridge branch opened on 4 July 1904. This station was in Belmont Road and served until December 1938

23 Inaugural train of the Uxbridge branch photographed at Ruislip on 4 July 1904. Although the branch was intended for multiple-unit electric trains, it was worked by steam for six months

24 This new station of modern design near Uxbridge High Street (on a site previously occupied by old cottages) was planned in 1936, and opened on 4 December 1938. It also served Piccadilly Line trains, which had been extended to Uxbridge on 23 October 1933, shortly after the formation of London Transport. This view was taken in July 1958

25 A typical suburban train of the Metropolitan Railway near Willesden Green in the 1890s

26 Six-coach train headed by 'E' class steam locomotive at Neasden in 1905

27 'K' class locomotive on 'main-line' train, including a Pullman coach

28 One of the first (1864) batch of 'A' class 4-4-0 tank locomotives with original weatherboard outside Edgware Road engine sheds

29 'G' class 0-6-4 tank locomotive built in 1916 for express passenger work. There were only four of the type, and they were exceptional in being named

30 Camel-back electric locomotive No. 1, built in 1905, and designed to haul steam passenger and goods trains over electrified lines. The first ten were of this pattern, but the second ten had a box-like body

31 The early electric locomotives were replaced in 1922-23 by twenty new and more powerful units as seen here

32 ABOVE LEFT Rear view of the first multiple-unit electric stock of the Metropolitan Railway on a trial trip on 13 December 1904. The gate ends, unsuitable for working in the open air, began to be converted to end vestibules in 1906

33 ABOVE RIGHT Five-coach Circle stock at South Kensington in October 1950

34 ABOVE A train of new 'A 60' stock on the Amersham service in 1961

35 BELOW 'C 69' stock designed for Circle Line and Hammersmith & City workings, which began to replace older stock in 1970

36 and 37 Compartment stock for 'main-line' service on the Metropolitan, showing (left) first-class and (right) third-class accommodation. Compartment stock last ran in service on 5 October 1962

38 Interior view of 'C 69' stock in 1970. To give maximum passenger flow for the short-distance Circle passenger, the car is provided with four pairs of double doors each side

Inner Circle, but there were also sound reasons of traffic competition to be quoted in support of the conflicting views. Both railways were cultivating the expanding traffic of south-west London, which was developing as a prosperous residential district, and both had eyes on the once-important exhibition traffic at South Kensington. When it became obvious that the existing companies could not agree to build the missing link, independent City interests took the matter in hand and formed the Metropolitan Inner Circle Completion Railway Company, which was incorporated on 7 August 1874, but the money was not forthcoming from the public. In the words of *The Railway News* 'Sir Edward Watkin exerted all his influence to prevent the company raising the necessary capital, and his efforts were crowned with success'.

Nevertheless the Metropolitan realised that powerful forces were determined to see the completion of the Inner Circle, and eventually Sir Edward was induced to work more or less harmoniously with the District. The Metropolitan and District (City Lines & Extensions) Act of 11 August 1879 authorized the two existing railways to build an Aldgate to Mansion House link jointly and also an extension line from the neighbourhood of Aldgate to effect a junction with the East London Railway at Whitechapel. Parliament intended to prevent all further friction between the Circle companies, and Section 89 of the Act required that 'each of the two companies shall, for the purpose of securing to the public the advantage of the continuous working of the said Inner Circle with the other portions of the two companies' lines, work over the railways of the other company forming part of such Inner Circle'. This mandate continued unrepealed until after the formation of London Transport, so that the Inner Circle service had the unusual distinction of being maintained under statutory obligation. Even after the compromise, the Metropolitan was 'awkward'. It rushed forward its own line to Tower Hill (under its unexpired powers) and there built a temporary station called The Tower of London within three nights and two days, which was opened on 25 September 1882. Watkin continued to offer obstruction by causing the South Eastern Railway to raise objections to the works near Cannon Street Station, and also in regard to the Whitechapel extension.

The City Lines & Extensions were brought into public use on 6 October 1884, when the Inner Circle at last became a reality. In addition, both Metropolitan and District trains began to work over the East London Railway, the Metropolitan from Hammersmith (Met.) to New Cross (S.E.R.) *via* the northern part of the Circle, and the District from Hammersmith to New Cross (L.B.S.C.R.) *via* the southern part.

In order to tell a consistent story of the development of the Metropolitan as an urban railway, and also as one providing terminal facilities in the City of London for the suburban trains of main-line railways, only brief mention has been made of a change in policy whereby it aspired to become a main-line railway. As early as 1874, when the 'Extension line' consisted only of a single track from Baker Street to Swiss Cottage, Sir Edward Watkin revealed to the shareholders his desire that the Metropolitan should 'break through the iron barrier which . . . larger railways had constructed around you . . . and connect your great terminus with Northampton and Birmingham and many other important towns'. Where he envisaged the great terminus is uncertain, but, earlier in the same year, he had spoken of an hotel scheme at Moorgate Street Station, including also shops, a restaurant, and offices. We have seen how the 'Widened Lines' provided additional tracks for Great Northern and Midland trains into Moorgate Street, and a new link called the Smithfield curve (between Snow Hill and Aldersgate Street) had been opened on 1 September 1871, giving direct access for London, Chatham & Dover trains from the south. (The last-named curve remained in use until 1 April 1916).

Although this particular scheme came to nothing, Watkin continued to have the 'main-line' idea in mind. In 1853 he had become General Manager (and later Chairman) of the Manchester, Sheffield & Lincolnshire Railway, and continued his association with that railway throughout the remainder of his business career. On becoming Chairman of the Metropolitan, he appointed John Bell as Secretary of the company (on 17 October 1872) and thereafter the two worked together closely until Watkin's virtual retirement in 1894. Bell, who had succeeded Myles Fenton as General Manager at the beginning of 1880, became Chairman of the Metropolitan on 5 May 1894, and held that office until 28 November 1901, a few months after Watkin's death. Nevertheless, Bell told a Parliamentary committee in 1899 that Watkin 'did not confide his policy to many people' and apparently he himself knew little of his plans. It seems probable that secrecy was not the only reason, but rather that many of Watkin's activities might be characterised more as expediency of the moment than as consistent long-term policy. In July 1888 he told the Metropolitan shareholders: 'I do not intend to be satisfied, if I live a few years, without seeing the Metropolitan Railway the grand terminus for a new system of railways through England.'

The Metropolitan continued to push out into the country, and in the light of subsequent events, the further prolongations have been referred to as if they were portions of a predetermined plan, but this is far from being the case. The Rickmansworth extension was a Metropolitan promotion, authorised by Act of 6 August 1880, but the Aylesbury & Rickmansworth was a separate company formed on 18 July 1881, and apparently was not in origin a Metropolitan scheme. The sections were opened from Harrow to Pinner on 25 May 1885; to Rickmansworth on 1 September 1887; and to Chesham on 8 July 1889.

By this time a fairly definite scheme had been propounded for the extension of the Manchester, Sheffield & Lincolnshire Railway to London, with the aid of the Metropolitan. The Aylesbury & Buckingham Railway, a local line linking Aylesbury with Verney Junction which had been opened on 23 September 1868 and worked by the Great Western, was vested in the Metropolitan by Act of 25 July 1890. The further section of Metropolitan construction from Chalfont Road (later Chalfont & Latimer) was opened on 1 September 1892 to a terminus in Brook Street, Aylesbury. On 1 January 1894 the two were linked in Aylesbury joint station, and the G.W.R. handed over the working of the Aylesbury & Buckingham Railway on 31 March. The Metropolitan thus reached a point at Verney Junction which was just over 50 miles from Baker Street, but it was served at first by local Metropolitan trains. The through service from Baker Street was begun on 1 January 1897 when the Aylesbury & Buckingham had been double-tracked.

Meanwhile, the M.S. & L.R. had secured its Act on

28 March 1893 for its London extension, more than 90 miles of new line from Annesley to join the Metropolitan at Quainton Road. An agreement of 18 December 1890 had given the M.S. & L.R. running powers over the Metropolitan from Quainton Road to Baker Street, and Watkin had a vision of a great trunk railway from Lancashire and Yorkshire through London to the South Eastern Railway, and thence to Dover and by means of a Channel Tunnel (another scheme with which he was associated) to the Continent of Europe. However, the M.S. & L.R. became dissatisfied with the idea of Baker Street as its London terminus and secured Parliamentary approval to build its own station at Marylebone, approached by a new line from Canfield Place (near Finchley Road). The M.S. & L.R. changed its name to the Great Central Railway in August 1897 and this, the last main-line railway to London, was opened for coal traffic on 26 July 1898, and for passengers on 15 March 1899.

Another line in which the Metropolitan became interested at this time was the Oxford & Aylesbury Tramroad, extending for some 6½ miles from Quainton Road to Brill. This had been built in 1870-72 as the Wotton Tramway by the Duke of Buckingham, without Parliamentary powers and mainly on his own land, to serve his estate, but it carried public traffic. From 1883 onward it became involved in schemes for extension to Oxford, and a company called the Oxford & Aylesbury Tramroad took over the working on 15 October 1894. It secured some new rolling stock, but never acquired the freehold and made no new line. With the coming of the Great Central to London, the Metropolitan arranged to take over the working of the line to Brill on 1 December 1899, and thereafter it was referred to as the Brill branch, but it retained its rural aspects and was never extended.

By the turn of the century the Metropolitan thus had one foot in the main-line camp as well as its basic underground system in London. Under the revised arrangements with the Great Central, the Metropolitan had agreed to quadruple its line from Canfield Place to Harrow, to give the Great Central the exclusive use of two tracks. These were built as far north as Preston Road, where a temporary junction was made, but delay in delivery of girder work for bridges deferred the completion of the four tracks to Harrow until 31 March 1901. A further change was that the Metropolitan lines north of Harrow came under the management of a Metropolitan & Great Central Joint Committee on 2 April 1906.

The urban underground lines, with a growing volume of traffic, presented the problems associated with steam operation in a confined space. Electric traction had been considered in the early 1880s but a combination of lack of funds and the uncertain economics of such traction at the period caused the matter to be deferred. Obviously track electrification involved agreement with the District, in view of the combined ownership of the Inner Circle. Relationships between the two companies became less tense after the resignation of Sir Edward Watkin in 1894 as a result of his incapacitation by a stroke. The two companies experimented by equipping with third rail on the direct-current system the Earl's Court to High Street line (fed by a small temporary power station at Earl's Court) at a cost of £20,000. Tests began in February 1900, and public traffic was carried from 21 May to 6 November at first at the 'novelty' fare of 1s. single, and subsequently at normal fares. Three coaches of the six-coach train (with Siemens motors) were owned by each railway. Eventually, the District and the Metropolitan set up a joint committee which recommended the adoption of the three-phase a.c. 3,000-volt system (with overhead conductor wires) developed by Ganz of Budapest.

In February 1901 the Metropolitan accepted the recommendation, but the whole matter was thrown into the melting pot by a change in the control of the District. The dominating personality in the American group which took over was Charles Tyson Yerkes (1837–1905) of Chicago. Yerkes was entirely out of sympathy with the relatively untried Ganz system of electrification; he favoured low-voltage direct current as already in use on the Central London Railway and used extensively in the U.S.A., whereas the Metropolitan wished to adopt the joint committee recommendation. The matter was referred to arbitration, which began before the Hon. Alfred Lyttelton K.C. on 7 October 1901. After a 12-day hearing the arbitrator's award was given on 11 December in favour of the District. The result was a triumph for Yerkes, and the electrification was undertaken on American lines. Yerkes offered to take over the Metropolitan on lease at a guaranteed fixed and perpetual dividend of 3½ per cent., but this was refused.

The Metropolitan introduced its first multiple-unit electric service on 1 January 1905 between Baker Street and Uxbridge. This included a newly-built branch from Harrow to Uxbridge, which was opened on 4 July 1904, but worked by steam for six months. Then followed the Aldgate to Whitechapel section on 1 July 1905, at first for the Ealing-Whitechapel service of the District Railway. The Metropolitan began an Inner Circle electric service on 1 July 1905, but withdrew it the same day and then worked Aldgate–Baker Street–South Kensington electric, at first from 10 a.m. to 5 p.m. and all day from 24 July. The actual Circle electric service was introduced gradually from 13 to 24 September. The line between Edgware Road and Hammersmith was worked electrically from 5 November 1906, and the branch between Latimer Road and Addison Road was converted at the same time. Electric traction between Rayners Lane and South Harrow began on 1 March 1910, when the District Railway used it to extend its own service to Uxbridge. The spur had been built in 1904, but remained without public service for six years because of one more disagreement between the two companies. Although owned by the Metropolitan it never carried a passenger service of the owning company. The East London Railway was worked electrically from 31 March 1913, with the Metropolitan providing the passenger service.

The system of electrification adopted was similar to that of the District, namely, 600-volt direct-current. Third and fourth rails were used, with the positive 16 in. outside the track (and 3 in. higher) and the negative in the centre, 1½ in. higher than the running rails. The new electric rolling stock was of the open saloon type, but compartment stock continued to be used on the 'Extension line', hauled by electric locomotive over the electrified tracks and thence by steam locomotive. Experimental haulage of steam trains by electric locomotives began in the summer of 1906 and from 1 November of that year all trains north of Baker Street were hauled electrically. Neasden generating station was built by the Metropolitan and opened on 1 December 1904. It was closed on Sunday, 21 July 1968, at which time it was the last in Great Britain to supply electricity at $33\frac{1}{3}$ cycles.

Electrification on the 'Extension line' went no further than Harrow until after the First World War, but from 1 November 1906 all Chesham, Aylesbury, and Verney Junction trains from Baker Street were hauled by electric locomotive as far as Wembley Park, thus covering the tunnel section. Harrow became the principal locomotive change point on 19 July 1908. Electric traction was extended from Harrow to Rickmansworth on 5 January 1925. The latter place then became the change point, and indeed remained so until 9 September 1961, when Amersham became the terminus of Metropolitan Line trains. After the introduction of electric traction, a few through trains were run to the City over the single-line junction at Baker Street from 28 January 1907, but regular two-way services did not begin until 1 July 1909 after some track modification. Even so, there was no double-track connection until 4 November 1912. This was constructed as part of a long overdue rebuilding of Baker Street Station undertaken in 1911. The 'centre stone' was laid with some formality on 24 July 1912, and the major work completed by the end of 1913, but the war delayed the finishing touches, and some features were not brought into use until 1923.

Although for much of its independent career of just over 70 years, the Metropolitan strove to be regarded as one of the main-line railways of the country, it never quite achieved such recognition. Yet a railway on which a Pullman service was run from Aylesbury and Chesham to Liverpool Street and Aldgate offered a facility that exceeded what is normally regarded as urban transit. The Pullman cars *Mayflower* and *Galatea* ran from 1 June 1910 until 7 October 1939 and were the first electrically-hauled Pullmans in Europe.

Under the American auspices which had obtained control of the District Railway, and had built the Bakerloo, Piccadilly, and Hampstead tubes, a new and dynamic personality came on the scene with the appointment in 1907 of Albert Henry Stanley (1874-1948) later Lord Ashfield, as General Manager of that group. An early important step which he is said to have inspired was the use of a distinctive symbol for all the underground railways in London whether within his own group or not. This was adopted at a meeting of the London Passenger Traffic Conference on 29 February 1908 and took the form of an illuminated sign bearing the word UNDERGROUND with large initial and final letters, which thereafter was exhibited at all stations and survives, with slight modification in design, as the symbol of the London Transport railways. In 1909 the District also began to make its station name signs more distinctive (amidst numerous advertisements) by showing them in white letters on a blue panel behind which was a solid red disc. The Metropolitan took a similar step with its station nameboards from May 1915, but using a red diamond. At the same time the Metropolitan introduced the distinctive word 'Metro-Land' in its publicity for the beautiful residential areas served by its 'Extension line'.

To meet the needs of a rapidly growing traffic, particularly to the outer suburban area, arrangements were made to build two additional tracks. This quadrupling was brought into use from Finchley Road to near Kilburn on 30 November 1913, and thereafter in sections as available. By 31 May 1915 all sections to Wembley Park were opened, but war delayed further progress. These additional tracks enabled fast trains to be worked, which were impeded only by the Baker Street to Finchley Road bottleneck.

In the space available, it is impracticable to record all the changes in station names which have been made, but mention should be made of the omission of the word 'Street' from the titles of the City stations. It began in common usage, and even in railway publicity, during the first World War, but official dates are 26 January 1922 for Farringdon Street to become Farringdon & High Holborn (Farringdon only from 21 April 1936); Aldersgate Street became Aldersgate & Barbican in 1923 (and Barbican only on 1 December 1968); and Moorgate Street simply Moorgate from 24 October 1924.

At the end of 1925 a scheme was devised for relieving the Baker Street to Finchley Road bottleneck by constructing a new line in a 15 ft. 6 in. tube from a point near Kilburn & Brondesbury Station to Edgware Road Station on the Inner Circle. Edgware Road Station was rebuilt in 1926, but the large tube to accommodate Metropolitan rolling stock was never made. A further step towards improving the access of

'Extension line' trains to the City was taken in 1926 when the dead end of the derelict tunnel west of King's Cross, built in 1868 but never used, was extended about 220ft. and linked with the eastbound Circle line. An electrified track was laid, and some tracks of the 'Widened Lines' to Moorgate were also equipped, so that electric trains could use the terminal platforms at Moorgate. This was brought into use on 15 March 1926. As the new link was unidirectional its value was limited, but it continued in use until 27 April 1935, when the rebuilding of King's Cross Circle Line station on a new site caused it to be abandoned. The new King's Cross was brought into use for the first time on 14 March 1941.

No further extension of electrification was made under Metropolitan Railway auspices, but two branches were built for electric traction from the outset. That from Moor Park to Watford (a joint venture with the L.N.E.R.) was opened on 2 November 1925. The other was the swan song of the Metropolitan, namely, the branch from Wembley Park to Stanmore, which was opened on 10 December 1932, but since 20 November 1939 has been served only by Bakerloo Line trains. Government assistance in raising capital for new works enable the four-tracking of the 'Extension line' to be continued, and it came into full use as far as Harrow on 10 January 1932. Meanwhile, a burrowing junction at Harrow had been opened on 14 September 1925, to avoid conflicting paths of main-line and Uxbridge branch trains.

With the establishment of the London Passenger Transport Board by Act of 13 April 1933, the Metropolitan Railway together with the District Railway and its associated tube railways, the principal bus undertakings, and both company and municipal tramways, came under unified ownership from 1 July 1933. The Metropolitan had been one of the chief opponents of the scheme (in large measure because it still regarded itself as a main-line railway) but eventually terms had been arranged and were approved by the Metropolitan stockholders on 14 July 1932. In the changed circumstances much of the old individuality necessarily disappeared. Main-line aspirations ceased for ever and an important and comprehensive scheme of improvements and electrification extension was announced in November 1934. This included additional tracks between Harrow and Rickmansworth; station reconstruction; electrification from Rickmansworth to Amersham; and the provision of a Bakerloo tube link between Baker Street and Finchley Road. The last-named proposal was regarded as the alternative to the 1925 scheme to relieve the bottleneck.

Implicitly, this involved the ultimate abandonment of operations beyond Amersham, and as early as 14 May 1935 Mr. Frank Pick told a Committee of the House of Commons that London Transport could not be expected to run suburban services to Aylesbury. The first closure was the Brill branch from Quainton Road, on which the last trains ran on 30 November 1935. The passenger service between Quainton Road and Verney Junction ceased on 4 July 1936, and Waddesdon Station on the main line was closed at the same time. (Goods traffic to Verney Junction continued until 6 September 1947.)

Then London Transport, which had taken over 36 steam locomotives from the Metropolitan, arranged to discontinue its own operation of steam locomotives for passenger trains, and on 1 November 1937 the London & North Eastern Railway took over the steam working beyond Rickmansworth (and 18 Metropolitan steam locomotives), hauling London Transport coaches between Rickmansworth and Aylesbury. The L.N.E.R. also took over 270 goods wagons and agreed to operate the goods traffic heretofore maintained by the Metropolitan. London Transport, however, kept some steam locomotives for another 34 years for use on works trains and for shunting in depots. Electric locomotives continued to be employed to haul through trains to the changeover point, and also to haul Great Western trains between Paddington and Aldgate. The latter workings ceased on 16 September 1939.

The new works were well in hand at the outbreak of war in 1939, but the need to conserve resources of labour and material caused many of the Metropolitan improvements to be suspended in November 1939. The Bakerloo tube link between Baker Street and Finchley Road, with intermediate stations at St. John's Wood and Swiss Cottage, was opened on 20 November 1939 and Bakerloo trains were extended to Stanmore, taking over the whole working of that branch. At the same time, the Metropolitan Line stations at Lord's (the new name given to St. John's Wood on 11 June 1939) and Marlborough Road were closed. But for the outbreak of war, Lord's Station would have been retained for access to the world-famous M.C.C. cricket ground. Metropolitan Line platforms at Swiss Cottage were taken out of service on 18 August 1940. From 1 February 1940 only one class accommodation (in effect abolishing first class) was provided on all L.T. trains, excepting those to Aylesbury and Watford.

At nationalization on 1 January 1948, the London Passenger Transport Board became part of the British Transport Commission, but worked as a distinct unit by the London Transport Executive. It took over responsibility for the erstwhile Metropolitan & Great Central line from Harrow to Aylesbury, and for the Chesham and Watford branches. In 1955 the pre-war plans were modified in the light of changed conditions. Electrification from Rickmansworth to Amersham and Chesham was opened to public service on 12 September 1960.

Metropolitan Line through services last ran to stations north of Amersham on 9 September 1961, and thereafter London Transport ceased to operate locomotive-hauled public trains. The furthest outposts of the system therefore were Amersham 23·9 miles from Baker Street, and Chesham 25·7 miles. By this time the provision of additional tracks was well in hand, and sections were brought into use as available. The work was finished on 16 June 1962, and the modernization of the Metropolitan Line complete. New aluminium saloon-type rolling stock was introduced, and compartment stock last ran in service on Friday, 5 October 1962. The last batch of compartment stock had been ordered in 1931 by the Metropolitan Railway; none under London Transport auspices.

When the British Transport Commission was dissolved as from 1 January 1963, London Transport reverted to its original status of an independent Statutory undertaking, and was called the London Transport Board. As such it celebrated the centenary of the Metropolitan with a noteworthy commemorative run on 24 May 1963, when, to the surprise of all, the Lord Mayor of London (Sir Ralph Perring) acted as motorman throughout the journey from Paddington to Moorgate. A plaque to mark the 1863 opening was unveiled at Baker Street the same day.

At the request of the Corporation of London, to facilitate the redevelopment of the heavily war-damaged Barbican area, London Transport realigned its railway between Moorgate and Aldersgate stations. The old curved route was replaced by a straight line in a reinforced-concrete covered way. The changeover took place in two stages. The new 'Widened Lines' used by trains of the London Midland and the Eastern Regions of British Railways, were brought into use on 21 June 1965, and the new Circle lines on 6 December 1965. Moorgate Station, which sustained severe war damage and was restored only on a temporary basis, is now being rebuilt as part of a comprehensive commercial development scheme.

Another important change affecting the City of London (although just outside its boundary) was the building of the new Tower Hill Station on a site to the east of the old one (which had been named Mark Lane until 1 September 1946). The new station, opened on 5 February 1967, is on the site of the temporary Tower of London Station built in haste by the Metropolitan in 1882 and used for only two years.

A further change in the status of London Transport came on 1 January, 1970. Under the Transport (London) Act 1969, Parliament dissolved the London Transport Board and set up the London Transport Executive in its place, giving overall financial and policy control to the Greater London Council and with London Transport retaining responsibility for management of the undertaking and the day-to-day operation of the red bus and Underground services.

Until 1971 a small fleet of tank locomotives kept steam alive on the Metropolitan as they hauled works trains and shunted in the depots. To replace Metropolitan engines that had reached the end of their useful life, of which the last was scrapped in 1963, London Transport secured ex-Great Western 0–6–0 pannier tanks, and it was three of these that last worked. When their duties were taken over by three Rolls-Royce/Sentinel 325 h.p. diesel-hydraulic 0–6–0 locomotives, the last day of steam locomotive operation was marked on Sunday, 6 June 1971, by a commemorative run from Moorgate to Neasden depot. The train was headed by one of the ex-Great Western engines, and thus the first and last steam trains on the world's first underground railway were hauled by Great Western locomotives.